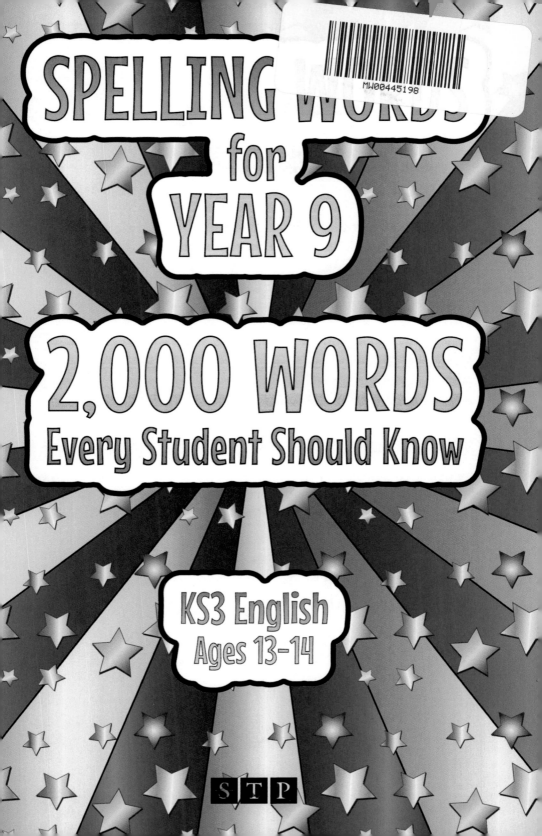

ABOUT THIS BOOK

Using a **fresh approach** to spellings lists, this illustrated collection of Spelling Words is designed **to make spelling fun** for students whilst ensuring they master essential spelling rules covered by the end of Year 9.

Containing **2,000** carefully selected **level-appropriate** words, this book is made up of **70** Themed Spellings Lists that

- Have **brightly-coloured illustrated backgrounds** and **engaging titles**
- Cover **loads of topics** that **actually interest students** such as Space Exploration, Adobe® Photoshop®, & Zombies
- Relate to other **areas covered at school** including computer science, finance & economics, & Shakespearean English
- Target **key words that students overuse in their formal writing** (e.g. 'analyse', 'consequently', & 'disagree')
- Quietly introduce **specific areas of spelling** that students need to know (e.g. Greek & Latin roots, word building, and homophones & near homophones)
- Are made up of **25 to 30 words each**

HOW TO USE IT

All the **lists are self-contained**, so you can work through them **in order**, or, you can dip in to use them for **focused practice**. And, as these lists are themed, they are **also a useful resource** for a range of **writing projects and exercises**.

For your convenience, an **Index** to the **spelling rules, patterns, and themed areas** dealt with by each of the lists is included at the **back of the book** on page 40.

Published by STP Books
An imprint of Swot Tots Publishing Ltd
Kemp House
152-160 City Road
London EC1V 2NX

www.swottotspublishing.com

Text, design, illustrations and layout © Swot Tots Publishing Ltd
First published 2021

Swot Tots Publishing Ltd have asserted their moral right under the Copyright, Designs and Patents Act, 1988, to be identified as the author of this work.

Typeset, cover design, and inside concept design by Swot Tots Publishing Ltd.

British Library Cataloguing-in-Publication Data. A catalogue record for this book is available from the British Library.

ISBN 978-1-912956-41-8

CONTENTS

CONTENTS Cont.

In Literary Terms...

anastrophe
anthropomorphism
aphorism
asyndeton
chiasmus
colloquialism
double entendre
innuendo
leitmotif
litotes

malapropism
meiosis
polysyndeton
tautology
tricolon
antinovel
Bildungsroman
burlesque
caricature
commedia dell'arte

courtly love
epigram
epigraph
epitaph
epithet
eulogy
parody
roman-à-clef
satire
sonnet sequence

EGOMANIA & CO.

Anglomania
anthomania
automania
bibliomania
demonomania
dipsomania
discomania
egomania
Francomania
gamomania

hypomania
infomania
kleptomania
megalomania
melomania
micromania
monomania
mythomania
nostomania
onomatomania

opsomania
phytomania
plutomania
poriomania
pseudomania
pyromania
sitiomania
sonnettomania
technomania
zoomania

The Roots Of The Matter 1

synaesthesia
synaesthete
synaesthetic
synapsis
synchronicity
synchronous
synchrony
syncopate
syncretise
syncretism

syndactyly
syndrome
synergy
syngamy
synonym
synonymity
synonymous
syntax
synthesis
synthesiser

syllogism
symbiosis
symbiotic
symmetry
sympathy

People Who...

costermonger
fellmonger
fishmonger
ironmonger
newsmonger
phrasemonger
rumour-monger
scandalmonger
scaremonger
warmonger

wordmonger
blacksmith
coppersmith
goldsmith
gunsmith
ironsmith
locksmith
silversmith
songsmith
tinsmith

tunesmith
whitesmith
wordsmith
cartwright
millwright
playwright
ploughwright
shipwright
wainwright
wheelwright

Up And Down

assurance	optimism	disconsolation
assuredness	positiveness	dispiritedness
bullishness	positivity	downheartedness
buoyancy	sureness	fatalism
certainty	defeatism	forlornness
certitude	dejection	gloominess
confidence	depression	glumness
conviction	desolation	hopelessness
enthusiasm	despair	melancholy
hopefulness	despondency	pessimism

Urbanite/Ruralite?

bustling	polluted	fertile
congested	sprawling	georgic
cosmopolitan	suburban	idyllic
gridlocked	teeming	pastoral
metropolitan	urban	picturesque
municipal	agrarian	provincial
non-rural	agricultural	rugged
overbuilt	Arcadian	rural
overcrowded	bucolic	rustic
overpopulated	depopulated	sylvan

Con-junction Box

accordingly	en masse	namely
appositely	equally	nevertheless
collectively	erroneously	notwithstanding
comparatively	evidently	rightfully
concurrently	hence	simultaneously
consistently	henceforth	singularly
contemporaneously	hereafter	thereafter
conversely	indeed	thereby
correspondingly	likewise	thus
elsewhere	mistakenly	undoubtedly

Crime Wave

armed robbery	espionage	libel
arson	forgery	manslaughter
assault	fraud	modern slavery
blackmail	harassment	mugging
bribery	hate crime	murder
burglary	high treason	rape
cybercrime	hijacking	slander
domestic abuse	hostage-taking	terrorism
drug trafficking	human trafficking	theft
embracery	kidnapping	trespass

Behind Bars

approved school
borstal
brig
concentration camp
death camp
detention centre
dungeon
gaol
guardhouse
Gulag

house of correction
jail
labour camp
lock-up
panopticon
penal colony
POW camp
prison camp
remand centre
can

chokey
clink
cooler
slammer
the nick

Sch-opping List

schadenfreude
schedular
schema
schematic
schematically
schematisation
schematise
scherzando
scherzo
scherzos

schism
schist
schizoid
schizophrenia
schizophrenic
schlepp
schlump
schmaltz
schmooze
schnapps

schnitzel
scholastic
schooner
schtick
schwa

Double Trouble

cribbage
gibbet
gobbet
lobbyist
ribband
scribbler
addendum
additives
addressable
adducible

rudderless
sodden
foppery
kappa
opportune
rappel
steppes
suppositional
diarrhoea
ferrous

garrulous
haemorrhage
parricide
scurrilous
admissible
dissimilitude
dissolution
impressionistic
intercession
unprepossessing

Lit Crit

medieval
Renaissance
Restoration
Augustan
Neoclassical
Enlightenment
Regency
Romantic
Gothic
Transcendental

Victorian
Pre-Raphaelite
Naturalism
Realism
existentialism
Modernism
postmodernism
cultural materialism
deconstruction
feminism

Marxism
New Criticism
new historicism
postcolonialism
post-structuralism
psychoanalysis
queer theory
reader-response theory
Russian Formalism
structuralism

Hate Is A Strong Word

abhorrence	loathing	execrable
animosity	odium	loathsome
antipathy	rancour	abhor
aversion	repugnance	abominate
detestation	revulsion	deplore
enmity	abhorrent	deprecate
execration	abominable	detest
hostility	deplorable	execrate
ill feeling	deprecative	loathe
ill will	detestable	recoil

SILENT, BUT DEADLY I

pneumatic	psyche	psychometric
pneumonia	psychedelic	psychopath
pneumonic	psychiatric	psychopathic
psalm	psychiatrist	psychosis
psalmist	psychiatry	psychotic
psalter	psychic	
pseudo	psychobabble	
pseudonym	psychodrama	
pseudoscience	psychologist	
psoriasis	psychology	

Pandemon–ium!

atrium	euphonium	podium
auditorium	harmonium	premium
cerium	ilium	primordium
colloquium	imperium	proscenium
consortium	lithium	sanatorium
delirium	medium	scriptorium
dominium	moratorium	sensorium
effluvium	opium	solarium
emporium	palladium	symposium
epithalamium	pandemonium	tedium

There In Spirit

astral projection	levitation	séance
aura	mediumship	second sight
clairvoyance	parapsychology	sixth sense
conjuration	phantasm	spectral
cryptozoology	precognition	spiritualism
demonic possession	preternatural	supermundane
ectoplasm	psychokinesis	telaesthesia
exorcism	psychometry	telepathy
extramundane	retrocognition	transcendental
extrasensory perception	scepticism	ufology

Vowelless

crypt	lynx	scry
cyst	myrrh	Sphynx
dryly	myth	spryly
fly-by	nymph	sylph
glyph	pry	sync
gym	psst	synth
gypsy	psych	thymy
hymn	pygmy	tryst
lymph	pyx	wryly
lynch	rhythm	wynd

QED

aggregate	corollary	Pythagorean
algebraic	differential	quadrant
algorithm	equation	quadrilateral
array	exponential	quotient
asymmetrical	extrapolation	radical
axiom	irrational	rhombus
computational	logarithm	simultaneous
concentric	matrix	tangential
congruent	Platonic solids	theorem
coordinate	progression	trigonometry

Happy Endings I

barrister	huckster	protester
broadcaster	jester	punster
chorister	jokester	quester
contester	jouster	quipster
enlister	mobster	requester
forecaster	molester	rhymester
fraudster	newscaster	taster
gangster	poetaster	trickster
harvester	pollster	tryster
hipster	prankster	waster

Body Language

abdominal	digestive	renal
alimentary	frontal	respiratory
arterial	gastric	spinal
bronchial	hepatic	synaptic
cardiac	metabolic	vascular
cardiovascular	nervous	
cerebral	neural	
circulatory	oesophageal	
colonic	pancreatic	
coronary	pulmonary	

Head-Scratchers

file	mean	staid
phial	mien	stayed
gamble	packs	throes
gambol	pax	throws
greave	pearl	tire
grieve	purl	tyre
jewel	rouse	vial
joule	rows	vile
levee	roux	white
levy	rue	wight

'Wh' The Whimsical

whackiest	whetted	whirlybird
whammies	whey	whiskered
wharfs	whiffle	whist
wharves	Whig	whit
wheedle	whiling	whittle
wheeling	whimsical	
whelp	whimsy	
wherewithal	whippersnapper	
wherry	whippet	
whetstone	whirligig	

15

This Neck Of The Woods

arboretum
botanical garden
canopy
coppice
copse
foliage
grove
hothouse
spinney
thicket

woodland
arboreal
biennial
coniferous
deciduous
evergreen
flowering
hardy
indigenous
medicinal

ornamental
pendulous
perennial
tropical
variegated

Silver-Tongued

articulate
communicate
convey
enunciate
express
formulate
pronounce
utter
verbalise
vocalise

voice
cogent
coherent
communicative
comprehensible
eloquent
expressive
fluent
intelligible
lucid

silver-tongued
unfaltering
well-articulated
well-expressed
well-spoken

To Sum Up...

abridge	summarisation	nutshell
distil	summary	outline
encapsulate	summation	overview
recap	summing-up	précis
summarise	synopsis	résumé
synopsise	abstract	round-up
abridgement	compendium	rundown
distillation	conspectus	shorthand
encapsulation	curriculum vitae	snapshot
recapitulation	digest	summa

Shocking!

ammeter	electrode	resistor
amps	electromagnet	rheostat
anode	filament	series circuit
capacitor	insulator	short circuit
cathode	ohm	storage
circuit board	ohmmeter	supercapacitor
circuit breaker	parallel circuit	transformer
circuit diagram	potentiometer	transistor
conductor	rectifier	volt
diode	relay	watt

Happy Endings II

froward
spaceward
untoward
wayward
windward
airward(s)
coastward(s)
downward(s)
earthward(s)
eastward(s)

forward(s)
heavenward(s)
homeward(s)
inward(s)
landward(s)
northward(s)
onward(s)
outward(s)
poleward(s)
rearward(s)

riverward(s)
seaward(s)
shoreward(s)
skyward(s)
southward(s)
sternward(s)
sunward(s)
toward(s)
upward(s)
westward(s)

In The History Books

abolitionism
alliance
assassination
assimilation
colonialism
foreign policy
geopolitics
imperialism
indirect rule
liberalism

nationalism
overseas empires
peacemaking
reconstruction
secession
unification
the American Civil War
the Boxer Rising
the Cold War
the Depression

the Indian Mutiny
the Opium Wars
British Raj
Democrats
Republicans
League of Nations
capitalism
communism
fascism
socialism

Loanwords

de rigueur
entente cordiale
faux pas
fin de siècle
force majeure
haute couture
in extremis
in medias res
in toto
ipso facto

jeu d'esprit
joie de vivre
la dolce vita
magnum opus
modus operandi
non sequitur
nouveau riche
objet d'art
pièce de résistance
pied-à-terre

plat du jour
prima facie
pro rata
raison d'être
savoir faire
sine qua non
sui generis
tour de force
vis-à-vis
vox populi

Quin-te-SS-en-C-e

associational
associative
assonance
classicist
crosspiece
disassociation
dissection
dissector
dissemblance
disservice

disseverance
dissidence
dissociate
dissociation
dissociative
dissonance
incessancy
issuance
ossicle
ossification

puissance
quintessence
reassociated
reassurance
reconnaissance

Has A Thing For...

ailurophile
arctophile
astrophile
audiophile
autophile
bibliophile
cartophilist
cinephile
coleopterist
deltiologist

dipterist
discophile
galanthophile
hippophile
lepidopterist
logophile
musicophile
mycophile
neophiliac
notaphilist

numismatist
oenophile
oologist
philatelist
phillumenist
Russophile
scripophile
technophile
turophile
xenophile

Got Your Money's Worth?

assets
bankruptcy
cash flow
collateral
credit rating
debt
depreciation
dividends
expenses
hedge fund

insolvency
interest rate
investment
investors
leverage
liability
loan
loss
mortgage
percentage

profit
rally
recession
repayment
revenue
shareholders
shares
solvency
stocks
vested interest

The Ends

bathe	rathe	tithe
blithe	reclothe	unclothe
breathe	scathe	unsheathe
clothe	scythe	wreathe
enswathe	seethe	writhe
enwreathe	sheathe	
inbreathe	soothe	
lathe	sunbathe	
lithe	swathe	
loathe	teethe	

SHY & RETIRING

demure	self-deprecating	unpresuming
diffident	self-effacing	unpresumptuous
docile	submissive	unpretentious
humble	subservient	unresisting
inhibited	timorous	withdrawn
introverted	unaggressive	
meek	unassertive	
reserved	unassuming	
reticent	unobtrusive	
retiring	unostentatious	

All Puffed Up

arrogant
boastful
bombastic
conceited
condescending
disdainful
egotistic
haughty
hubristic
immodest

lordly
opinionated
overbearing
pompous
pretentious
prideful
proud
scornful
self-important
smug

snobbish
supercilious
superior
swaggering
uppity

Ex Marks The Spot

exactitude
exclusivity
exemplar
exhilarating
expansive
expeditious
extemporise
extermination
extinguishable
extracurricular

ambidextrous
anorexia
contextualises
dexter
inexorable
inextricable
lexicography
overexposure
reflexive
unexpurgated

apex
circumflex
cortex
duplex
googolplex
multiplex
retroflex
Semtex
telex
vortex

Linguisticalities

abbreviation
acronym
antonymous
archaism
backronym
buzzword
byword
catchword
cognate
coinage

connotation
demotic
denotation
descriptor
discourse marker
etymon
false friend
homograph
hypernym
hyponym

initialism
lexicon
lexis
loanword
locution
neologism
nomenclature
nonce word
palindrome
toponym

Seeing It Both Ways

detachment
disinterest
egalitarianism
equitableness
equity
even-handedness
impartiality
neutrality
objectivity
open-mindedness

balanced
clinical
detached
disinterested
dispassionate
equitable
even-handed
fair-minded
impartial
neutral

non-discriminatory
non-partisan
objective
unbiased
unprejudiced

Judgement Calls

adjudge
adjudicate
analyse
appraise
arbitrate
assess
classify
criticise
deduce
derive

determine
estimate
evaluate
judge
weigh
adjudgement
adjudication
analysis
appraisal
arbitration

assessment
classification
criticism
deduction
derivation
determination
estimation
evaluation
judgement
rating

Soldiering On

Anzac
batman
bombardier
cavalryman
commando
crusader
digger
fighter pilot
foot soldier
fusilier

GI
grenadier
guardsman
gunner
infantryman
lancer
leatherneck
legionary
marine
militiaman

paratrooper
sapper
scout
sentry
sepoy
shogun
squaddie
storm trooper
Tommy
trooper

The Dogs Of War

air strike	carpet bombing	combative
blitzkrieg	decimation	hawkish
genocide	fusillade	hostile
massacre	incursion	martial
trench warfare	offensive	militant
annihilation	onslaught	militaristic
barrage	salvo	pugnacious
battery	skirmish	truculent
blitz	bellicose	warlike
bombardment	belligerent	warring

Profuse, Or Paltry?

abounding	liberal	negligible
abundant	plenteous	niggardly
ample	prodigious	paltry
bounteous	profuse	scanty
bountiful	prolific	scarce
copious	exiguous	skimpy
cornucopian	inadequate	sparing
exuberant	inappreciable	sparse
galore	insubstantial	stingy
lavish	meagre	wanting

A, B, C...

abstractionism	beguile	cadaverous
abysmal	benign	calligraphy
Alzheimer's	bequeath	camaraderie
ambience	berserk	carcinogen
anticlimactic	blasphemy	censorious
antihistamine	blazon	clandestine
apocryphal	boisterous	claustrophobic
apoplexy	bovine	commiserate
apostasy	bureaucracy	conglomeration
assimilate	bursary	contemporaneous

...X, Y, Z

Xanadu	yardage	zoologist
xebec	yashmak	zealotic
xenon	yearningly	zestiest
xenophobe	yeomanry	zeugmatic
xenophobia	yodelling	ziplock
xenophobic	yogi	zombielike
xerography	yonder	zonk
xi	youngling	zoomorph
xylem	Yuletide	zooplankton
xylograph	yuppify	zygotic

THE ROOTS OF THE MATTER II

appease
appeasement
appeaser
append
appendage
appendix
apperception
apperceptive
applicability
applicable

application
apportion
apportionable
appreciable
appreciate
appreciation
apprehend
apprehensible
apprehension
approachability

approachable
appropriate
appropriations
approximate
approximation

To Infinity & Beyond!

aeronautics
aerospace
artificial satellite
asteroid
astronautics
capsule
cargo
colonisation
comet
deep space

docking
extragalactic
galactic
gravitational field
module
moon landing
orbital
outer space
payload
planetary

pressurised
probe
propulsion
shuttle
space observatory
space station
spacewalk
supersonic
trajectory
unmanned

Ex-Ter-Mi-Nate!

android
antigravity
artificial intelligence
black hole
blasters
clones
colony
cyberpunk
cyborg
death ray

exoskeleton
extraterrestrial
force field
hyperspace
intergalactic
interplanetary
interstellar
kryptonite
Martian
multiverse

quantum
sentient
space-time continuum
subspace
technocracy
teleportation
terraform
tractor beam
warp speed
wormhole

Silent, But Deadly II

anachronism
anachronistic
asynchronous
catachresis
christen
chromatic
chromatography
chrome
chromium
chromosomal

chromosome
chronic
chronicle
chronicler
chronologically
chronologist
chronology
chronometer
chrysalid
chrysalis

chrysanthemum
diachronic
lachrymal
lachrymose
monochromatic
monochrome
ochre
sepulchre
synchronic
synchronise

I'LL BE BOUND

earthbound	southbound	muscle-bound
eastbound	spellbound	port-bound
fogbound	stormbound	pot-bound
housebound	westbound	rock-bound
inbound	windbound	town-bound
northbound	car-bound	
outbound	desk-bound	
outrebound	homeward-bound	
paperbound	ice-bound	
snowbound	iron-bound	

Not THAT Amazon

biodiversity	taxonomy	gastropod
commensalism	fauna	detritivore
decomposition	flora	insectivore
ecosystem	genus	invertebrate
erosion	phylum	vertebrate
habitat	species	endemic
infrastructure	algae	feral
life cycle	arthropod	prehensile
mutualism	crustacean	diurnal
predigestion	cryptozoa	nocturnal

Partiality & Prejudice

biased	partial	partiality
bigoted	partisan	partisanship
discriminatory	predisposed	predisposition
dogmatic	prejudiced	prejudgment
hidebound	bias	prejudice
inequitable	bigotry	
intolerant	discrimination	
intransigent	inequity	
one-sided	intolerance	
parochial	parti pris	

(In)Flexible

adamant	strict	cooperative
determined	stringent	flexible
obdurate	uncompromising	obliging
obstinate	unswerving	persuadable
resolute	unwavering	protean
resolved	accommodating	relaxed
rigid	adaptable	relenting
rigorous	amenable	tolerant
severe	complaisant	versatile
stiff	compromising	yielding

Ye Olde English I

ague	disport	propinquity
alack	eke	puissant
asunder	foe	redolent
avaunt	forfend	slay
beauteous	fourscore	smite
bethink	malapert	steed
betide	maugre	ween
betwixt	orison	whilom
contemnible	pelf	yclept
contumely	perish	yesteryear

Ye Olde English II

alarum	caitiff	marry
antick	canker	methinks
aroint	capon	peradventure
as lief	certes	prithee
baseborn	clepe	shrift
basest	cozen	sirrah
bawd	forsooth	swain
belike	gramercy	sweetmeat
beshrew	haply	tidings
bewray	lustre	troth

Dial P for Poison

Agent Orange	hydrogen cyanide	potassium cyanide
arsenic	hydrogen fluoride	prussic acid
arsine	lead monoxide	ratsbane
atropine	mercuric chloride	sarin
benzene	mercuric oxide	silver nitrate
carbon disulphide	methanol	sodium cyanide
carbon monoxide	methyl bromide	strychnine
cyanic acid	mustard gas	thallium
cyanide	nerve gas	vinyl chloride
formaldehyde	nitrogen dioxide	zinc chloride

Branded!

Astroturf	Photoshop	Uber
Auto-Tune	Ping-Pong	Velcro
Band-Aid	Rollerblade	Xerox
BubbleWrap	Scotch Tape	Yo-Yo
FaceTime	Sellotape	Zoom
FedEx	Skype	
Google	Super Glue	
Hoover	Tarmac	
Jet Ski	Taser	
Mace	Tipp-Ex	

Z Is For...

zabaglione
zakat
zany
zapper
zealot
zealous
zeitgeist
zemindar
Zen
zenith

zephyr
Zeppelin
zeroing
zestiness
zeta
zeugma
ziggurat
zilch
zillion
Zinfandel

zinnia
zircon
zither
zucchini
zygote

THE WORKS

artwork
basketwork
brickwork
brushwork
clockwork
footwork
framework
fretwork
groundwork
guesswork

handiwork
lacquerwork
latticework
legwork
metalwork
needlework
network
paintwork
passagework
patchwork

plasterwork
schoolwork
scrollwork
steelwork
stonework
teamwork
trelliswork
waxwork
wickerwork
woodwork

That's Stellar!

acclaim	panegyric	laud
accolade	plaudits	proclaim
adulation	applaud	commendable
approbation	celebrate	commendatory
blandishments	commend	esteemed
citation	emblazon	estimable
commendation	endorse	eulogistic
encomium	eulogise	laudatory
endorsement	extol	meritorious
kudos	hail	panegyrical

Coming Under Fire

admonishment	excoriation	excoriate
animadversion	remonstration	fulminate
aspersions	reprehension	lambast
castigation	reproof	pillory
censure	admonish	rebuke
chastisement	berate	reprimand
condemnation	castigate	reprove
denigration	chastise	scold
denunciation	chide	upbraid
disparagement	disparage	vilify

On The Face Of It

deface	surface	facelift
defacement	surfacing	face mask
efface	face down	barefaced
effacement	face up	faceless
interface	facet	shamefaced
interfaced	facetious	ashen-faced
outface	dogface	moon-faced
outfaced	boldface	red-faced
preface	typeface	whey-faced
prefacing	facecloth	white-faced

Txting

A3	DM	Njoy
AFAIK	FC	NRN
AFK	FWIW	OFC
ATM	GMTA	OMW
B4	ICYMI	ROFLOL
BAK	IDK	RUOK
BBL	IFYWIMAITYD	SMH
BRB	IMHO	SOHF
CMIIW	MSG	Ti2GO
CUL8R	NBD	XOXO

Arabian Delights

admiral
adobe
alcove
alfalfa
almanac
arsenal
assassin
azimuth
benzoin
cipher

elixir
erg
falafel
fennec
garble
harem
henna
jinn
loofah
mohair

monsoon
nadir
popinjay
ream
saffron
sequin
sherbet
tamarind
tariff
tarragon

Yea, Or Nay?

accord
accordance
concord
concurrence
congruence
congruency
congruity
consensus
consent
consonance

harmony
in concert
unanimity
uniformity
unison
altercation
clash
conflict
contestation
contradiction

controversy
debate
discord
disputation
dissensus
dissent
divergence
friction
opposition
rejection

Coax Vs Curb

coax	persuade	dehort
embolden	prevail on/upon	deter
encourage	prompt	disadvise
enjoin	spur	discourage
entice	sway	disincline
goad	urge	dissuade
impel	advise against	inhibit
incite	check	restrain
induce	curb	talk out of
influence	dampen	warn against

Computer Says, 'No'

3D printer	hard disk	router
central processing unit	hard drive	scanner
disk drive	inkjet printer	solid-state drive
dongle	laser printer	sound card
drive	memory card	thumb drive
expansion card	memory stick	trackball
expansion slot	modem	trackpad
flash drive	monitor	USB stick
flatbed scanner	motherboard	webcam
graphics card	processor	wireless mouse

It's Been Photoshopped

adjustment layer	eyedropper	palette
aliasing	filter	panorama
anti-aliasing	Gaussian blur	radial blur
bounding box	gradient	raster
clone	greyscale	resampling
composite	halftone	saturation
constraining	handle	scaling
cropping	hue	swatches
crystallize	lens flare	vector
diffuse glow	opacity	vignette

(Im)Precision

careless	shoddy	methodical
casual	sketchy	meticulous
cursory	slapdash	painstaking
desultory	slipshod	particular
half-hearted	superficial	punctilious
imprecise	assiduous	scrupulous
inaccurate	conscientious	sedulous
inattentive	conscionable	strenuous
lax	diligent	studious
negligent	fastidious	thorough

Z.. Z.. ZOMBIES!

anthropophagus
apocalypse
cadaver
cannibalism
cataclysm
consumption
corpse
devouring
festering
flesh-eating

gore
infection
invasion
mutation
necrosis
ooze
outbreak
pathogen
putrefaction
putrid

reanimated
repugnant
rigor mortis
rotting
survival
survival of the fittest
the living dead
the walking dead
virus
wormy

THAT'S A PROPER WORD?!

antimacassar
babushka
bellwether
boondoggle
borborygmus
chatoyant
cornucopia
curmudgeon
fugacious
gizzard

imbroglio
inglenook
kirtle
lackadaisical
medusal
orotund
persimmon
quiddity
rainmaker
sobriquet

stupefaction
Svengali
taradiddle
technobabble
tintinnabulation
veracious
widdershins
wisenheimer
yackety-yak
yonks

INDEX

In the following entries, the letter 'A' refers to the upper list on the page, while 'B' refers to the lower one.

Made in the USA
Monee, IL
03 October 2023

43939921R00026